TORONTO TRAVEL GUIDE

Where to Go & What to Do

STEPHANIE MASON

No part of this publication may be reproduced, stored in a retrieval system, or transmitted, in any form or by any means without the prior written permission of the publisher, nor be otherwise circulated in any form of binding or cover other than that in which it is published and without similar condition being imposed on the subsequent purchaser. If there are any errors or omissions in copyright acknowledgements the publisher will be pleased to insert the appropriate acknowledgement in any subsequent printing of this publication. Although we have taken all reasonable care in researching this book we make no warranty about the accuracy or completeness of its content and disclaim all liability arising from its use.

Copyright © 2019, Astute Press
All Rights Reserved.

Table of Contents

Toronto..7
   Customs & Culture..7
   Geography...8
   Weather & Best Time to Visit...9

Sights & Activities: What to See & Do...........................11
   CN Tower..11
   Casa Loma..12
   Hockey Hall of Fame...13
   Yonge-Dundas Square..13
   Nathan Phillips Square..14
   Air Canada Centre..15
   Roger's Centre...15
   Fort York...16
   Royal Ontario Museum...16
   Ontario Science Centre...17
   Art Gallery...18
   Museum of Contemporary Canadian Art......................19
   Toronto Islands..19
   Canada's Wonderland...21
   Toronto Zoo...22
   Ontario Place...23

Budget Tips..24
   Accommodation...24
      Alexandra Hotel..24
      Ramada Plaza Downtown Toronto...........................25
      Glen Grove Suites & Condominiums–The Maple Leaf........25
      Knights Inn...26
   Restaurants, Cafés & Bars...26
      Grand Electric..26
      Five Guys Burgers & Fries......................................27
      GUU Japanese Restaurant.......................................27
      Sneaky Dee's..28
      Nazareth Ethiopian Restaurant................................28
      Church Aperitivo Bar..29
   Shopping..29
      Eaton Centre..29
      Kensington Market...30
      St. Lawrence Market..30
      Yonge Street...31

Know Before You Go...32
   Entry Requirements...32

Health insurance	32
Travelling with Pets	33
Airports	33
Airlines	36
Hubs	36
Money Matters	37
Currency	37
Banking-ATMs	37
Credit Cards	38
Tourist Tax	38
Claiming Back VAT	39
Tipping Policy	39
Connectivity	39
Mobile Phones	39
Dialing Code	40
Emergency numbers	40
General Information	40
Public Holidays	40
Time Zones	41
Daylight Savings Time	42
School Holidays	42
Trading Hours	42
Driving Policy	43
Drinking Policy	43
Smoking Policy	44
Electricity	44
Food & Drink	44
Useful Websites	45

Toronto

Toronto is the largest city in Canada and the capital city of Ontario. Known as the "Big Smoke" and sometimes as the New York of Canada, Toronto is a fascinating center of culture, art and entertainment. Like its American counterpart, Toronto is a fast-paced and bustling city.

With a population of roughly 3 million, the city is part of the Greater Toronto Area (GTA), which itself is home to over 6 million people.

The city has gained popularity in recent years as one of the most culturally and ethnically diverse cities in North America. Toronto is not just a melting pot, it is a mosaic of cultures from all over the globe.

You can expect anything and everything from a city like Toronto. There are music festivals, good beaches, parks, sports venues, museums and a myriad of restaurants, bars and nightclubs to choose from. Whether you're staying for a just few days or a year, there is never enough time to fully experience all that Toronto has to offer, so soak up as much of the excitement as you can while you're here.

Customs & Culture

Statistically speaking, Toronto (pronounced "Tuh-ron-no" by Canadians) is second only to Miami for having the highest percentage of foreign-born residents, with more than half of its residents being born outside of the country. However, while Miami's immigrant population consists primarily of Cubans and Latin Americans, that of Toronto represents over 80 ethnicities, with no single predominant culture.

This multiculturalism is reflected in the city's many festivals, concerts, museums, shops, markets, restaurants, ethnic neighbourhoods, and public services. Ambling around, you will notice the multilingual street signs.

You may come across a Caribbean Carnival, a film festival, or a Shakespeare production in High Park.

You may pass through Chinatown, Kensington Market, Greek Town, Korea Town, Roncesvalle, Corso Italia, Little Italy, Little India and Little Jamaica and Little Portugal, among other neighborhoods.

Likewise, many public services boast their ability to provide services in several languages. Most banks can service Torontonians in English as well as varieties of Chinese and Italian or other languages prevalent in the area. If you run into trouble, Toronto's 9-1-1 emergency services are prepared to respond in over 150 different languages.

Geography

Toronto is located at the heart of the GTA, or Greater Toronto Area, and is part of a larger region known as the Golden Horseshoe, which stretches around Lake Ontario and also touches parts of Lake Erie and Georgian Bay. The city can be divided into 6 zones or boroughs: Old Toronto (which includes Downtown, the West End, the East End, Midtown and the Islands), Etobicoke (pronounced "A-toe-bi-koe"), York, East York, North York and Scarborough.

Servicing the GTA are 3 airports, the chief of which is Toronto Pearson International Airport, 30-50 minutes from the downtown core. There is also Billy Bishop Toronto City Centre Airport, more commonly known as "The Island Airport", which handles regional flights only, and Hamilton International Airport. Budget travelers may also want to look into flights to and from Buffalo-Niagara International Airport. Though it is across the border, Megabus runs from downtown Toronto to the airport, and flights tend to be cheaper, so it is a viable option.

There are several options you may want to consider for getting around Toronto. The city is very large, but traffic can be heavy during rush-hour, and taxis and parking fees expensive, so the frugal traveler should consider public transportation. The subway system is straightforward, quick and efficient, though with only 4 lines it may not meet all your needs. Thankfully, there is also a bus system, streetcar system, quasi-subway line and regional train, and bus system called GO Transit. The buses, streetcars and subway are all part of the TTC (Toronto Transit Commission). Single fares are usually $2.50-$3.00, though express and lengthier trips will cost more. Depending on the length of your visit and how often you plan to be using public transportation, you may want to consider a daily ($10.50) or weekly ($37.50) TTC pass. Weekly GTA passes are $54.

Weather & Best Time to Visit

Toronto does not suffer very harsh winters like the rest of the country, thanks to its location in the South near the American border. You can expect high temperatures in the wintertime to hover around freezing (0° Celsius or 32° Fahrenheit), and nightly lows of around -5 degrees Celsius (23°F). There are, however, bouts of colder weather coming in from the North, and snowstorms mixed with ice and rain are not uncommon, often disrupting traffic and other travel schedules. Consistent with the rest of the country, the coldest month is January but snowfall can occur anytime from November to mid-April, so come prepared with warm clothing and waterproof boots or shoes. Though cold and sometimes dreary, the winter can be enchanting and seem to cast some sort of spell with its crisp blankets of snow.

On the contrast, the summer months can get quite hot and humid. Daily highs average out at around 27 degrees Celsius (80°F), not including humidity, and nightly lows around 18 (65°F). Hotter days, peaking in the mid-30s, are becoming more and more common.

August and September are the wettest months due to thunderstorms, but the springtime brings a considerable amount of rain as well. Though Toronto's vibrancy extends even through the winter, late spring/early summer and early fall are considered to be the best times to visit. During this time, the temperatures are comfortable and the crowds are small, with the peak tourist season being mid-summer.

Toronto has something to offer in every season, with attractions and events year-round. Whenever you decide to come, there's sure to be more than a few things to enjoy.

Sights & Activities: What to See & Do

Depending on how long you will be in Toronto, and how many sights you want to see, you may want to consider getting the Toronto CityPASS. This gives you 43% off select attractions, and allows you to skip most lines. The pass costs a total of $69.50 and grants access to the CN Tower, Toronto Zoo, Casa Loma, Ontario Science Centre and the Royal Ontario Museum. Purchase your pass at the zoo's box office or online at www.citypass.com.

CN Tower

www.cntower.ca
301 Front Street West, Toronto, Ontario M5V 2T6
(416) 868-6937

Classified in 1995 as one of the Seven Wonders of the Modern World, the CN Tower is the icon which defines Toronto's skyline. It was originally built in 1976 in order to respond to existing transmission towers problems in the city. Today, towering at over 553 meters (over 1,815 ft.), it is Toronto's centre of telecommunications, serves over 16 Canadian television and FM radio stations, and, as the tallest free-standing structure in the Western hemisphere, is an internationally renowned architectural symbol.

At 346 meters (1,136 ft.), the LookOut Level offers an astonishing view of the city. If you're not satisfied, though, the SkyPod level offers a 360° perspective at 447m (1,465 ft.) high overlooking the city, Lake Ontario and beyond.

For a discounted price, buy your tickets online. Tickets for the LookOut Level are $27.50 for adults, and the SkyPod level will cost you an additional $12.00. The CN Tower is open every day of the year, with the exception of Christmas Day, from 9 a.m. to 10 p.m. though hours may change seasonally.

For the more daring individuals, an EdgeWalk experience has recently been introduced. For the hefty price of $175.00, you can walk outside around the roof's circumference (while harnessed) and literally get a bird's eye view of the city, not to mention a wicked photo. Another feature for the high-roller is 360, the revolving restaurant near the top of the tower. 360 is the epitome of extravagance. With the purchase of a main course, access to the LookOut and Glass Floor is included. For both these experiences, make sure you book a reservation well in advance.

Casa Loma

http://casaloma.org/
1 Austin Terrace,
Toronto, Ontario
M5R 1X8
(416) 923-1171

Located in midtown, Casa Loma is Toronto's castle. Though construction was halted in 1914 due to the start of World War I, Sir Henry Pellatt purchased the land and commissioned construction in 1911 for the largest private residence in Canada, with a total of 98 rooms.

CN Tower Toronto CA 2023 (bobistraveling, CC BY 2.0)

Architect E.J. Lennox, was responsible for the design of the mansion, as well as several other landmarks around the city. In 1933, the city seized Casa Loma for over $27,000 in back taxes, and in 1937 it was opened as a museum. Today, it is undergoing an exterior restoration.

Casa Loma is open daily from 9:30 a.m. to 5:00 p.m., and is closed only on Christmas day. General admission for adults is $20.55.

Hockey Hall of Fame

http://www.hhof.com/
Brookfield Place, 30 Yonge Street, Toronto, Ontario M5E 1X8
(416) 360-7765

It is difficult to describe the love that Canada has for hockey. It is much more than the pastime that gets Canadians through unforgiving winters; it is a pinnacle of national pride and identity. So it was only natural that, following the opening of several other halls of fame, Captain James Sutherland started a motion that hockey should have its own to call home.

Having argued that Kingston, Ontario was the birthplace of hockey, Sutherland convinced the NHL and CAHA (Canadian Amateur Hockey Association) to agree to establish a Hockey Hall of Fame in that city. The first members were inducted while plans were made and construction began. However, construction proved to be very costly, and after much delay, the NHL withdrew its support and decided to relocate the Hall of Fame in Toronto.

Today, General admission will run you $17.50, and true hockey fans will be glad to know that they can get their picture taken with the Stanley Cup for an additional $5.00 if the ticket is booked online.

Yonge-Dundas Square

http://www.ydsquare.ca/

Yonge-Dundas Square (commonly referred to as "Dundas Square" by locals) is a focal point for the downtown

Financial District, Toronto (Andrew Milligan sumo, CC BY 2.0)

community of Toronto. Aptly named, it is at the corner of Yonge Street, which was formerly the longest street in the world, and Dundas Street, and is an open public space that can also be used as a venue to accommodate some of the city's events. Most of these events are free, including concerts, receptions, films, theatrical events, and other promotions and celebrations.

The square came about after the city of Toronto launched a competition in 1998 for the design of a new square in order to reintroduce some of the old vitality into Yonge Street. Today, it offers an exciting yet serene scene at the heart of the city to sit and people-watch amidst the sometimes crazy downtown core. The square offers free Wi-Fi internet as well, and since it is public, it never closes.

Nathan Phillips Square

If Toronto is the New York of Canada, Nathan Phillips square is equivalent of the Times Square of Toronto. On New Year's Eve, you can watch the ball drop here alongside thousands of other people. Named after Nathan Phillips, who was the Mayor of Toronto from 1955 to 1962, it is located immediately in front of City Hall on the corner of Queen and Bay Streets, just a few blocks from Dundas Square.

Like Dundas Square, it is the host of many of the city's special events. One of the world's largest underground parking garages is located directly beneath the square, holding up to 2,400 cars. The square also showcases several sculptures and landmarks: the Freedom Arches, the Peace Garden, a statue of Sir Winston Churchill, and the reflecting pool which, in winter, is transformed into a public skating rink. A Speaker's Corner podium was also installed at the south west corner in an effort to promote free speech in Toronto. Anyone who wishes may express their opinions on camera, though, sadly, the recordings are no longer televised.

Air Canada Centre

http://

St Lawrence Market, Toronto (S. Rae, CC BY 2.0)

www.theaircanadacentre.com/

If you want an authentic Canadian experience, an NHL hockey game doesn't leave much to be desired.

Oddly enough, the NHL's Toronto Maple Leafs call the Air Canada Centre their home, and not the Maple Leaf Gardens. The Air Canada Centre is one of the country's leading venues for sports and entertainment, and has hosted over 2,000 events. Various other sports teams play at the centre as well, including the Toronto Raptors and the Toronto Rock Lacrosse Team. However, tickets can be steep, especially during the playoffs.

Roger's Centre

http://www.rogerscentre.com/
One Blue Jays Way, Toronto, Ontario M5V 1J3
416-341-1000 or 1-855-985-5000

If you're traveling on a budget but would still like to experience a live sports event in Toronto, a Blue Jays baseball game is your best option. Conveniently located downtown, next to the CN Tower, you can see a game at the Roger's Centre, formerly known as the SkyDome, for as little as $10.00. Different combination tickets are available online, such as the Grand Slam Combo for $39.00 which includes your ticket, food and beverages.

TORONTO TRAVEL GUIDE

St. Paul's Basilica (Ross Dunn: Thanks -10million views!, CC BY-SA 2.0)

Fort York

http://www.fortyork.ca/
250 Fort York Boulevard, Toronto, ON M5V 3K9
416-392-6907

Over 200 years ago, the huge city of Toronto was but a small community. Lieutenant Governor John Graves Simcoe, wary of the building tension between the British and Americans, ordered construction of a stronghold in 1793 in order to defend and control Lake Ontario. The provincial capital of Upper Canada was moved from Niagara Falls to Toronto, Toronto was renamed 'York', and a civilian settlement soon followed. A Government House was built as well as parliament buildings and a garrison east of modern day Bathurst Street. Simcoe's successor, Major-General Isaac Brock, strengthened the fort in 1811 in anticipation of conflicts.

In 1812, the Americans declared war and invaded Canada, and on April 27th, 1813, York was attacked. Several of the original buildings were burned or destroyed, but the British prevailed and rebuilt. Many of the buildings that you see today were built immediately after the war.

Today, Fort York's buildings are among the oldest in Toronto, and its walls surround the largest collection of original buildings from the War of 1812. The fort is operated as a museum, and is open 361 days a year. Admission for adults is $9.00, but the hours of operation vary, so make sure to check online when planning your visit.

Royal Ontario Museum

http://www.rom.on.ca/en
100 Queen's Park, Toronto, ON M5S 2C6

416.586.8000

By far, the most unique and unconventional museum in Toronto is the ROM. It is the country's largest museum of world culture and natural history. With a convenient downtown location, it attracts over one million visitors every year. The ROM boasts over 40 galleries, ranging in theme from fossils, to African art, to Canadian history, to clothing and interior design. It also features a crystalline-formed and originally controversial new entrance, "The Crystal".

The ROM's most eccentric feature, however, is its "Friday Night Live". Throughout May and June, the museum turns discotheque on Fridays after 7 p.m., and visitors can enjoy beverages and live music amongst dinosaurs and prestigious paintings. Tickets for these events are $12 and should be bought in advance on the museum's website.

Ontario Science Centre

http://

Toronto (Florian Dreyer, CC BY 2.0)

www.ontariosciencecentre.ca
770 Don Mills Road, Toronto, ON M3C 1T3
416-696-1000

When it first opened in 1969, the Ontario Science Centre was a pioneer for its unique hands-on approach to science. The centre differs from conventional museums in that the exhibits are not for display only; rather, they are mostly interactive. The exhibits feature just about every theme that can be found in science and in nature, ranging from anatomy to music, and from geology to astronomy, with some miscellaneous exhibits. Such exhibits have included "Happy Potter The Exhibition" and "Body Worlds", and the latest "Game On 2.0", an exhibition on the history of video games. The centre also has its own school, which offers credited University Preparation courses in various science subjects, and an IMAX theatre.

The Ontario Science Centre is open 7 days a week, 364 days a year (the exception being Christmas Day). Hours are 10 a.m. to 4 p.m. Monday to Friday, and 10 a.m. to 5 p.m. on weekends and holidays. General admission is $22.00 for adults.

Art Gallery

http://www.ago.net
317 Dundas Street West, Toronto, Ontario, M5T 1G4
1-877-225-4246 or 416-979-6648

This gorgeous, modern building is located in the downtown Grange Park district, and features the largest existing collection of Canadian art. It also showcases a considerable number of works from Europe, Africa and Oceania, and works from the Renaissance and Baroque eras. In addition to these galleries, the AGO also holds many sculptures, an extensive library, a gallery workshop space, a restaurant, research centre and lecture hall, among other features. It is open from 10 a.m. to 5:30 p.m. daily, but closed on Mondays. General admission is normally $19.50 for adults, but free on Wednesday nights from 6-8:30 p.m.

SIGHTS & ACTIVITIES: WHAT TO SEE & DO

Museum of Contemporary Canadian Art

www.mocca.ca
952 Queen Street West, Toronto, Ontario M6J 1G8
(416) 395-0067

The MOCCA features two large exhibition spaces dedicated to Canadian and international artists who address challenging topical issues.

The works showcased in this museum are always innovative and influential. Definitely worth a look, hours are Tuesday to Sunday, 11 a.m. to 6 p.m., and admission is a refreshing 'pay what you can'.

Toronto CN Tower (Open Grid Scheduler - Grid Engine, CC0 1.0)

Toronto Islands

http://torontoislands.org/

The Toronto Islands are a tranquil haven amongst a huge, bustling metropolis. They are made up of a chain of a dozen small islands, the largest of which are Toronto Island (or Centre Island), Middle Island, Ward's Island, Olympic Island and Algonquin Island. They are home to a small residential community, making them the largest urban car-free community in North America.

To reach the islands, you can take a ferry from the Ferrydocks at 9 Queen's Quay West, located south of Queen's Quay between Yonge and Bay Streets.

The ferry costs $7.00, including return, can accommodate recreational bicycles, and leaves approximately every 30 minutes on weekends and holidays (less often during the week). You can take a ferry either to Ward's Island, Centre Island or Hanlan's point. Whichever direction you choose to take, the ride lasts about 15 minutes each way. Water taxis are also available, but for a higher price. For more information on schedules, go to http://www.toronto.ca/parks/island/ferry-schedule.htm.

Once you arrive at your destination on any of the islands, you can rent a canoe, bicycle or quadracycle, play some disc golf, volleyball, tennis or softball, have a barbeque on one of the fire pits in the picnic areas, or simply just lie on the beach soaking up the sun and admiring the city skyline from a distance. If you happen to be in Toronto on a particularly beautiful day, it is a great way to escape the stresses of the city and just relax for the day.

Canada's Wonderland

https://

Toronto Exhibition Place (Open Grid Scheduler - Grid Engine, CC0 1.0)

www.canadaswonderland.com/
9580 Jane Street, Vaughan, ON L6A 1S6
(905) 832-8131

Canada's Wonderland, previously known as Paramount Canada's Wonderland, is the country's first and largest major theme park. One of the park's attractions is International Street, similar to the Walt Disney Parks'Main Street, U.S.A, with Latin, Scandinavian, Mediterranean and Alpine themed buildings.

In earlier years, the stores in this area sold high-quality imported goods in accordance with their themed buildings, and restaurants sold unconventional foods, also themed, such as shrimp, paella and smoked sausage.

The park also features a 20 acre waterpark, Splash Works, a Medieval Faire, Action Zone, Happyland of Hanna-Barbera area, Kidzville, Zoom Zone, and Planet Snoopy.

With a total of 68 rides including 16 roller coasters, and 11 water rides, Canada's Wonderland attracts over 3 million visitors per year. The most recent and renowned rides are Leviathan and Behemoth. At over 93 meters (306 feet), Leviathan is the tallest ride in the park and lasts almost three and a half minutes. Riders are dropped from the peak at an 80 degree angle, reaching speeds of 148 km/hr. Behemoth is known for its 180 degree hairpin turn and 2 helixes.

Tickets are $39.99 for adults when purchased online. With all its thrills and attractions, there's sure to be something for everyone at Canada's Wonderland.

Toronto Zoo

http://torontozoo.com
2000 Meadowvale Rd, Toronto, ON M1B 5K7
416-392-5929

The Toronto Zoo is one of the largest zoos in the world at 710 acres, and with over 10km of walking trails.

It is located near the Rouge River in Scarborough, about 30 minutes from downtown, and is accessible by public transit.

The zoo is home to over 5,000 animals representing over 500 species, which are divided into seven zoogeographic regions: Indo-Malaya, Africa, the Americas, Australasia, Eurasia, Canadian Domain and the Tundra Trek.

Highlights include a 5-acre Polar Bear habitat, a Gorilla Rainforest, and the Great Barrier Reef. There is also a special Discovery Zone, which features an interactive experience for children called the Kids Zoo, a two-acre water park called Splash Island, and the Waterside Theatre. General admission for adults is $28.00.

Ontario Place

http://

Toronto Subway (heather0714, CC BY 2.0)

www.ontarioplace.com/
955 Lake Shore Blvd W, Toronto, ON M6K 3B9
(416) 314-9900

Currently undergoing revitalization, Ontario Place is a multi-purpose site located on the shore of Lake Ontario, just south of Exhibition Place. It was opened over 40 years ago as a theme park of the same name which closed in 2011. It consists of three artificially constructed and landscaped islands.

Today, the Ontario Place Marino is still open, as well as The Molson Canadian Ampitheatre, Echo Beach, and Atlantis Pavilion.

Budget Tips

Toronto Waterfront (Open Grid Scheduler - Grid Engine, CC0 1.0)

Accommodation

Alexandra Hotel

http://alexandrahotel.com/
77 Ryerson Avenue, Toronto, Ontario M5T 2V4
(416) 504-2121

Specifically seeking to accommodate budget travelers who value convenience, the Alexandra Hotel is located at the heart of downtown Toronto, near the Kensington Market, Chinatown, Little Italy and the University of Toronto. Streetcars and subway stops are also within walking distance.

Each room comes equipped with one double bed and one twin bed, a private bath with full tub, a kitchenette, cable TV, internet and an individually controlled air conditioner and heater. The best feature of this hotel is that, with an average of $99.95 per night, its price is hard to beat.

Ramada Plaza Downtown Toronto

http://

View from CN Tower Toronto CA 2080 (bobistraveling, CC BY 2.0)

www.ramadaplazatoronto.com/
300 Jarvis Street, Toronto, ON M5B 2C5
1-855-247-4371

You can't get any closer to downtown than this. At 2 blocks from Yonge Street, a quarter-mile from the Eaton Centre, this high-rise is located in Toronto's Garden District, home to the city's Gay Village, Allan Gardens and several heritage buildings. If you happen to be visiting Toronto during its world-famous Pride celebrations, this is where you want to stay.

Amenities include a business center, indoor pool, spa tub, sauna, fitness facilities, and an on-site restaurant. All guestrooms have complimentary wireless Internet access, phones, cable TV, climate control and coffeemakers.

Glen Grove Suites & Condominiums–The Maple Leaf

http://www.glengrove.com/downtown/maple_leaf.htm
390 Queens Quay W Toronto, ON - M5V 3T1
416-489-8441 or 1-800-565-3024

At the heart of downtown Toronto, this beautiful condominium residence is within walking distance from the CN Tower, Skydome, and most other of the city's landmarks.

You are literally just steps away from the harbourfront, ferry docks and lake, parks, subways, theatres, restaurants and countless other attractions.

You can stay for a minimum of 3 nights at The Maple Leaf Quay, a state-of-the-art building complete with hot tub and sauna, fitness centre, billiards table and media room, meeting room, an indoor golf driving range, and rooftop seating with barbeque. Each room features a full kitchen with microwave and dishwasher, high-speed Wi-Fi, TV/DVD entertainment centre, complimentary Starter Pack which includes coffee, tea bags and other essentials, and a private phone with free local calls.

When you stay with Glen Grove, you really do have all the comforts of home for the price of an affordable hotel. Daily rates vary from $109-199, depending on time of the year and number of rooms you desire.

Knights Inn

http://knightsinntoronto.com/
117 Pembroke St, Toronto, ON, M5A2N9
1-866-299-2910

Knights Inn Toronto hotel is located right downtown, steps away from the Allan Gardens, and within walking distance to the Eaton Centre, Dundas Square, and many, many more attractions. The history property has been around since the York period, though its rooms have been newly renovated.

Its amenities feature free internet access, a microwave and fridge in the breakfast area, luggage storage, and best of all, complimentary continental breakfast. The entire property is smoke-free. Accommodation starts at the low price of $79.

Restaurants, Cafés & Bars

Grand Electric

http://www.grandelectricbar.com/
1330 Queen Street West, Parkdale, M6K1L4
416.627.3459

Located in Parkdale, west of downtown, this taco restaurant is famous for its fish tacos and bourbon selection. It is extremely informal, serves deliciously juicy and authentic food, and is unexpectedly cheap. They don't take reservations and they tell it like it is, which is part of the appeal. This place is open for lunch every day, and open for dinner from 5:30 p.m. until midnight or later. The vibe is a mix of relaxed and hearty, with some hip hop playing in the background and the sounds of loud laughter and chatter swirling about.

Though the chalkboard menu changes often, you can expect an assortment of tacos, burritos, appetizers and daily specials. If you're feelings adventurous and it's on the menu, try the beef cheek or pigs tail. Tacos are generally around $3 each, which for Toronto is very reasonable, and specials are usually around $10-$15.

Grand Electric is also revered for its drink selection; a huge assortment of bourbon, and delicious mixed drinks such as Horchada or Michelada. Though there can sometimes be a line out the door and down the block, the food and drinks at Grand Electric are certainly worth the wait.

Five Guys Burgers & Fries

http://www.fiveguys.com
329 Yonge Street, Toronto, ON M5B 1A1
416-591-0404

The Murrell brothers decided to open a burger joint in 1986 in Washington, DC. It quickly gained a following and expanded throughout the country. Today, Five Guys Burgers and Fries has several locations in Toronto, so if you happen to be outside the downtown core, take a look at their website for other locations. They use only fresh ingredients – nothing is ever frozen, only cooled – they use only peanut oil, and all menu items are trans-fat free. If you've got a hankering for some delicious comfort food, but want to be healthy, Five Guys is the way to go.

There are over 250,000 possible ways to order a burger at Five Guys, and you can take your fries plain or Cajun style. Prices are very affordable; a full meal will cost you $10-15.

GUU Japanese Restaurant

http://guu-izakaya.com/toronto/
398 Church Street Toronto, O.N. M5B 2A2

416-977-0999

Guu is a Japanese Izakaya restaurant, which is basically a bar that serves food along with its drinks. It is equipped with a full sake bar, and the food is interesting, to say the least. It is a delicious medley of authentic Japanese and contemporary taste, which somehow work harmoniously together. They are open for dinner and stay open late every day of the week.

Expect a bustling atmosphere and a friendly staff. Prices for most items are under $10.

Though the line-up can sometimes be long, the culinary experience at GUU is worth the wait.

Sneaky Dee's

http://sneaky-dees.com
431 College St., Toronto, ON M5T 1T1
(416) 603-3090

Sneaky Dee's is popular among students for its reasonable prices, lively and homey atmosphere, and connection to the music scene.

It opened its doors to the city in 1987 and hasn't looked back. Very much an integral part of Toronto's culture, it is also a concert venue which hosts a variety of different parties every week.

The food is pub and Tex-Mex style, and there is a different special every night of the week, from ribs and wings to pork sliders and fajitas. For an unforgettable nacho platter, get the King's Crown. No matter where you're from, you'll feel at home at Sneaky Dee's.

Nazareth Ethiopian Restaurant

969 Bloor Street W
Toronto, ON M6H 1L7
(416) 535-0797

Nazareth is an Ethiopian restaurant in Bloorcourt known for its delicious food, friendly staff, generous portions and low prices. Many Torontonians rave that this is the best Ethiopian food in town. There are only 8 items on the menu, but every single option will satisfy your taste buds. There is a vegetarian option which is extremely popular, even among meat-eaters.

Due to its popularity, you can expect line-ups, but platters are around $10 each and the portions are large enough to feed two. Beer is $4. At that price, it's hard to be disappointed.

Church Aperitivo Bar

http://churchaperitivobar.com/
1090 Queen Street West, Toronto ON
416 537 1090

You'd think that an Italian restaurant which offers a variety of carefully crafted cocktails, fine cuisine and a trendy atmosphere would be out of the question for the frugal traveler, but you'd be wrong. Church Aperitivo bar is very affordable, especially for its kind. Come on a Wednesday or a Friday from 5-7 p.m. or Saturday from 5-6:30 p.m. for delicious complimentary appetizers with the purchase of an equally delicious beverage.

Shopping

Toronto is well-known throughout Canada and beyond for its unbelievable shopping. With such incredible variety, you are sure to find whatever it is you're looking for.

Eaton Centre

http://www.torontoeatoncentre.com
220 Yonge Street, Toronto, ON, M5B 2H1
(416) 598-8560

At the heart of downtown Toronto, there is a mall which boasts over 320 shops, restaurants and other services.

The Eaton Centre is aptly named after the Eaton's department store which once anchored it. Conveniently located on the subway line ad connected to both Dundas and Queen Stations, the mall attracts over one million visitors per week, making it Toronto's number one tourist attraction.

The mall features Canada's largest store, the Hudson Bay department store, and interior passages that form part of Toronto's underground pedestrian network, PATH. It is enclosed by Yonge Street to the East, Queen Street West to the South, Dundas Street West to the North, and James Street and Trinity Square to the West. The Eaton Centre is an unexpected architectural and shopping gem not to be overlooked.

Kensington Market

www.kensington-market.ca

Kensington Market is by far the most vibrant and diverse part of Toronto. It is located just west of downtown and bordered by Spadina to the East, Dundas Street W. to the South, Bathurst Street to the West and College Street to the North. If you are already downtown, it is best to find Kensington on foot, though several street cars run through it.

The market is comprised of many shops, ethnic grocery stores, restaurants, bars, cafes and several art and entertainment venues. It has been designated a National Historic Site of Canada, and is also known for its Victorian style houses and buildings. In the early twentieth century, the area was populated mostly by eastern European Jewish immigrants and some Italians. It was one of the poorer areas of the city, and became known as the "Jewish Market", selling knickknacks and gifts reminiscent of Europe.

After the Second World War, most of the Jewish population moved North to the suburbs, which made room for a wave of new Caribbean and East Asian immigrants. Throughout the years, many refugees and other immigrants from troubled countries have made their way to the area, adding to its diversity. Additionally, Chinatown is located just East of Kensington.

Thanks to its narrow streets, Kensington is mostly a pedestrian area. You can stroll from shop to shop, discovering great finds and deals on clothing, furniture and a vast array of unique knickknacks and gifts.

St. Lawrence Market

http://www.stlawrencemarket.com/
92 - 95 Front Street East, Toronto

(416) 392-7219

The St. Lawrence Market was named the world's best food market by National Geogrpahic.

It has two different buildings: the St. Lawrence North and St. Lawrence South. The first hosts weekly farmer's markets and antique markets, and the latter hosts restaurants, a gallery, and a variety of shops, bakeries and delis. Free wireless internet is provided throughout the South Market.

The market is embedded deep in Toronto's history; it served at the city's first permanent city hall and jail house in the nineteenth century. Today, it is home to over 50 vendors of meat, cheese, fruits and vegetables on the first floor alone, The Market Gallery on the second floor, and a cooking school on the mezzanine floor. In total, there are over 120 vendors who enthusiastically display their life's passion.

Yonge Street

http://downtownyonge.com/

The construction of Yonge Street has been designated as an Event of National Historic Significance in Canada, as it was once the longest street in the world at 1,896 kilometres long (1,178 miles). It was an integral part of the planning and settlement of the city back in the 1790's. Starting at Queen's Quay and making its way through several major cities, including Vaughan and Markham, Yonge Street is often referred to as "Main Street Ontario", and was the site of Canada's first subway line.

Today, there are countless retailers, restaurants, bars and other businesses along Yonge Street. You can take in the essence of downtown Toronto while walking down the street, do some window shopping, and score some pretty exceptional deals.

Know Before You Go

Entry Requirements

To visit Canada as a tourist you will need a valid travel document, such as a passport, a certificate of good health and a clean record with absolutely no criminal convictions. Additionally, you may be asked to convince immigration officers of strong ties with your home country, your intent to leave at the end of your stay and your means to support yourself financially for the duration of your stay. In most cases, you will also need an entry document in the form of either a visitor visa or, in the case of citizens of countries that are visa exempt, an Electronic Travel Authorization (eTA). Visitors from the USA, members of the Royal Family and French residents of St. Pierre and Miquelon are the only persons exempt from needing an eTA. In the case of family groups, each family member will need to apply separately for an Electronic Travel Authorization. Countries exempted from requiring a visa include the United Kingdom (and British Overseas Territories such as Gibraltar, Pitcairn Island, the Falkland Islands, the Cayman Islands, Montserrat, Bermuda, the British Virgin Islands, St Helena, Anguilla, the Turks and Caicos Islands), Australia, New Zealand, Belgium, the Netherlands, France, Greece, Cyprus, Austria, Germany, Denmark, Finland, Sweden, Norway, Iceland, Spain, Portugal, Switzerland, Italy, Ireland, Hungary, Poland, the Czech Republic, Japan, Croatia, Slovenia, Slovakia, Latvia, Lithuania, Liechtenstein, Malta, Monaco, San Marino, Andorra, Samoa, Papua New Guinea, the Solomon Islands, Chile, the Republic of Korea and Singapore. A visitor's visa is valid for 6 months and you can apply to have this extended by 30 days.

Health insurance

Medical treatment can be expensive in Canada and the Canadian government does not offer any payment for medical treatment. There are no reciprocal agreements between Canada and the UK, the European Union or Australia regarding medical treatment. For this reason, visitors should make arrangements for sufficient health insurance to cover any medical emergencies as well as repatriation, if it is required, before leaving home. Temporary health insurance can be arranged through a

Canadian agency for a period of up to 365 days, with premiums starting at between $20 and $25. When considering insurance policies, do bear in mind that some extreme outdoor sports like skiing may not be covered automatically by your policy. If you are planning to participate in activities not normally covered, you should make arrangements for additional cover.

Travelling with Pets

When travelling with pets to Canada, the first requirement is the submission of proper travel documents. In the case of dogs, the animal will need to be inspected at the point of entry and a fee for this is levied at $30. All points of entry to Canada have an animal inspector on duty, which means that advance notification is not required.

Cats entering Canada do not need to be quarantined or microchipped, but they will need to be accompanied by a detailed rabies vaccination certificate or a health certificate stating that they are from a country recognized by Canada as rabies free. In the case of pets from the European Union, a pet passport will be accepted as alternative, provided it contains all the required details. Guide dogs and other assistance dogs are exempt from most of the restrictions that apply to other animal importations.

No import certificate is required for most reptiles and amphibians, with the exception of tortoises and turtles, in which case an application must be made a minimum of 30 days prior to import date to the Canadian Food Inspection Agency. Pet birds need to spend at least 45 days in quarantine, where a CFIA inspector will inspect their health. Application for quarantine must be made prior to your arrival in Canada. You will also need to make a declaration stating that the bird(s) have been in your possession for a minimum of 90 days and have not been in contact with other birds during that period. Birds originating from China, Vietnam, Bangladesh, Egypt, India and Indonesia are prohibited from entering Canada.

Airports

Toronto Pearson International Airport (YYZ) is the busiest airport in Canada in terms of passenger traffic. Located 22.5km northwest of Toronto's downtown area, it provides access to Toronto, the capital of

Ontario as well as the Golden Horseshoe, Canada's most populous region. Terminal 1, its primary terminal is one of the largest buildings of its kind in the world and its modern facilities are streamlined by the ThyssenKrupp Express Walkway, one of the fastest people-moving walkways in the world. The airport also has shops, a variety of eateries and free Wi-Fi coverage. A second airport serving Toronto is the **Billy Bishop Toronto City Airport** (YTZ), named after Canada's top flying ace from World War 1. It is located on an island in Toronto Harbour. From the airport, Toronto's CBD can be reached via a pedestrian tunnel from Eireann Quay or a scheduled ferry service. The airport falls under the Toronto Port Authority and is co-administered with the city's harbour. Besides three runways, there is also a base for seaplanes. Ontario's third major airport is the **Ottawa/Macdonald–Cartier International Airport** (YOW), the 6th busiest in Canada and 2nd busiest in the province. It serves Ottawa, but also offers connections to the bustling centers of Toronto and Montreal as well as a gateway to the Arctic.

Vancouver International Airport (YVR) lies on Sea Island in Richmond, about 12km from the downtown area of Vancouver City. Although planning for the airport began as early as 1929, the site first served as a Royal Canadian Air Force base during World War Two and the proposed civilian airport only became a reality after the war. As a Pacific Gateway, Vancouver International Airport provides non-stop connections to Asia and the International Terminal offers United States Border Preclearance facilities. The multi-award-winning airport welcomes visitors to Canada with a striking collection of Aboriginal art in the form of wooden sculptures and totem poles as well as the YVR Aquarium with over 800 marine species. Regular airport personnel are backed by a team of volunteers, trained to assist travellers in navigating their way through the airport. To aid the disabled, special wheelchair lifts have been installed and check-in counters have headsets for travellers with hearing disabilities. The rapid transit Sky Train connects to Vancouver's metro rail service. Vancouver International Airport also offers free Wi-Fi coverage. The second busiest airport in British Columbia is **Victoria International Airport** (YYJ), which offers access to Vancouver Island. Recently renovated, it has various features for disabled travellers, including wheel chair friendly facilities, large signage, phones with augmented transmission and relieving areas for service dogs. The airport is set in scenic surroundings and environmental management is a high priority.

Several of its ground vehicles are electrically powered and there is a bicycle assembly station just outside the main terminal as well as a bike path.

Montréal–Pierre Elliott Trudeau International Airport (YUL), formerly known as Montréal–Dorval International Airport, is located in the suburb of Dorval, about 20km from downtown Montreal. Utilized from the 1940s, it provides access to Montreal and Quebec, but can also serve as a gateway to parts of Ontario and even Vermont and New York in the USA. Like Vancouver, it offers United States Border Preclearance facilities, making it a modern and people friendly trans border terminal. Find your way around the airport easily with the YULi smartphone app. For easy access from the airport, a shuttle bus service connects travellers to the metro service to stops at Lionel-Groulx metro station, Central Station and Berri-UQAM metro station. **Halifax Stanfield International Airport** (YHZ) provides access to the mainland of Nova Scotia as well as its nearby maritime regions. **Winnipeg James Armstrong Richardson International Airport** (YWG) first opened in 1928 and is one of Canada's oldest airports. It is located about 10km from Winnipeg's downtown area and offers access to Winnipeg and the province of Manitoba. Additionally, it also serves as a gateway to the remote northern regions. One of its original hangars has been converted to an aviation museum, where visitors can view a collection of historical bush planes as well as Canada's first helicopter.

The province of Alberta is served by two large airports. **Calgary International Airport** (YYC) offers access to its most populous city and the majestic Canadian Rocky Mountains. First opened in 1938, it has entered a transitional phase with its new facilities scheduled for opening at the end of October 2016. If you have a few hours to while away, visit the Space Port, where you can enjoy simulated space flights or view artefacts on loan from NASA. **Edmonton International Airport** (YEG) is located about 26km from downtown Edmonton and offers a gateway to the Northern part of Alberta. Both Calgary and Edmonton have United States Border Preclearance facilities. **Kuujjuaq Airport** (YVP) is located about 2.8km southwest of Kuujjuaq in Quebec and provides access to the remote Nunavik region. It is a mandatory frequency airport, which means that it does not have sufficient air traffic to warrant a control tower.

Airlines

Air Canada is the flag carrier and largest airline in Canada. It was founded from Trans-Canada Airlines in the 1930s, renamed in the 1960s and privatized in the 1980s, following the deregulation of Canada's air travel industry. The service flies to over 100 international and domestic destinations and is linked by codeshare agreement to 28 other international airlines, including Lufthansa, United Airlines, Aegean Airlines, EgyptAir, Jet Airways, Turkish Airlines, Singapore Airlines, Air India, Air China, All Nippon Airways and Scandinavian Airlines.

WestJet is a Canadian budget airline that was founded in the mid-1990s. Currently it is the second largest carrier in Canada, flying up to 20 million passengers annually to over 100 destinations. The airline offers no-frills service and embraces environmentally sustainable strategies. Jazz Aviation is a regional service that connects passengers to over 75 destinations in Canada and the USA. Another budget airline is Sunwing Airlines, which is based in Toronto and was recently acquired by the US tour operator, Vacation Express. Perimeter Aviation is the largest regional aircraft carrier in Manitoba and offers connections to 23 destinations in Manitoba and Ontario. It also supports the region's medical evacuation services.

Air Inuit is collectively owned by the Inuit community of Nunavik and it offers connections to domestic destinations in Quebec, Nunavut, Newfoundland and Labrador. Calm Air is a regional service that provides regional connections between the northern parts of Manitoba and Nunavut. It is based at Thompson in Manitoba. Pacific Coastal Airlines connects travellers to destinations in British Columbia. Another regional carrier serving British Columbia is the family run Orca Airways.

Hubs

Toronto Pearson International Airport serves as the largest hub for Air Canada, but the airline also operates hubs at Montréal–Pierre Elliott Trudeau International Airport, where it is based, Calgary International Airport and Vancouver International Airport. Additionally, it has a strong presence at the international airports of Edmonton, Halifax, Ottawa and Winnipeg. The primary hub for the budget carrier WestJet is Toronto Pearson International Airport. Its second hub is at Calgary International

Airport, where it is based. WestJet also has a strong presence at Edmonton International Airport, Vancouver International Airport and Winnipeg James Armstrong Richardson International Airport. The primary base for Jazz Airline is at Halifax Stanfield International Airport. Jazz also has hubs at Vancouver International Airport, Calgary International Airport, Toronto Pearson International Airport and Montréal–Pierre Elliott Trudeau International Airport. Winnipeg James Armstrong Richardson International Airport and Thompson Airport serve as hubs for Perimeter Aviation. Kuujjuaq Airport is the main operating base for Inuit Air. Calm Air has two primary hubs at Thompson Airport and Winnipeg James Armstrong Richardson International Airport and secondary hubs at Churchill Airport in Manitoba and Rankin Inlet in Nunavut. Vancouver International Airport serves as the main hub for Pacific Coastal Airlines and also serves as a hub for Orca Airways.

Money Matters

Currency

The currency for Canada is the Canadian Dollar, which is often fairly close in value to the US dollar. The currency is available in denominations of $5, $10, $20, $50, and $100. Coins are issued in denominations of 5c (a nickel), 10c (a dime), 25c (a quarter), $1 (a loonie) and $2 (a toonie or twoonie). In 2011, Canada introduced the more resilient polymer bank note, which will eventually replace the paper bank note. At present, older paper notes are still in circulation and both types of notes are considered legal tender.

Banking-ATMs

You will be able to withdraw Canadian dollars from Automatic Teller Machines across Canada, but you should expect to pay a bank fee of $2 to $5, as well as a small percentage for the foreign currency transaction. If your bank is partnered with a Canadian bank, you can save on part of the fee. Bank of America, Barclays Bank in the UK, France, Spain and several African countries, Westpac in Australia, New Zealand, Tonga, Samoa and Fiji, Deutsche Bank, BNP Paribas and affiliate bank brands and Banca Nazionale del Lavoro in Italy are partnered with Scotiabank through the

Global ATM Alliance, which means that you will be able to save on some of the usual bank fees, although a percentage charge on foreign currency will still apply. Do remember to inform your bank of your travel plans before leaving home.

Credit Cards

Credit cards are widely accepted as legal tender across Canada. MasterCard and Visa are commonly accepted by most Canadian shops or businesses, although some travellers have reported problems with Visa in Canada. Walmart recently issued a statement that they will no longer accept Visa at their Canadian outlets, although they still accept MasterCard, American Express and Discover. Canada adapted to chip-and-pin credit card technology several years ago and you should experience no trouble using a card from the UK or European Union. Since financial institutions in Canada no longer accept liability for magnetic strip transactions, American visitors with older magnetic strips may experience difficulty using their credit cards as payment.

Tourist Tax

At present, Ontario is the only province in Canada that has not yet introduced legislation regarding hotel tax, but a number of cities in the province, such as Toronto, voluntarily collect what is termed as a destination marketing fee of 3 percent. In Vancouver 8 percent provincial tax plus 3 percent municipal tax is levied on hotel accommodation. St Johns in Newfoundland and Labrador levies a 4 percent tax on hotel rooms, while Gros Morne levies 3 percent. In Alberta, a hotel room tax of 5 percent is levied. In Quebec the rate varies, but is usually charged at $2 or $3 or 3 to 3.5 percent per night depending on the location of the accommodation. Winnipeg in Manitoba levies 5 percent, but exempts budget accommodation and hostels. Brandon in Manitoba also levies 5 percent, while Thompson levies $3 per night. Halifax levies 2 percent tax on larger hotels. In Charlottetown in Prince Edward Island, 2 percent tax is levied on tourist accommodation. Bathurst in New Brunswick adds $2 per night for accommodation, while Miramichi, Saint John and Charlotte County levy a municipal tax for tourists of 2 percent. Around Niagara Falls, 3 percent destination marketing fee is levied.

Claiming Back VAT

In Canada, the tax on purchases and services varies according to province. In Alberta, British Columbia, Manitoba, Nunavut, Northwestern Territories, Saskatchewan and Yukon, a goods and services tax rate (GST) of 5 percent applies. Ontario, Nova Scotia, New Brunswick, Prince Edward Island, Newfoundland and Labrador levy the so-called harmonized sales tax (HST), which combines federal and provincial taxes. The rate of HST is 13 percent in Ontario, New Brunswick, Newfoundland and Labrador, 14 percent in Prince Edward Island and 15 percent in Nova Scotia. Quebec levies 5 percent GST plus 9.975 percent Quebec Sales Tax. In 2007, Canada replaced the existing tax rebates for tourists and non-residents with the Foreign Convention and Tour Incentive Program (FCTIP), which limits rebates to taxes paid for tour packages or conventions. You are eligible if the amount spent exceeds $200 without the tax component and the supplier/tour operator has not yet refunded you through other channels.

Tipping Policy

In Canada, tipping is common practice and attitudes are generally similar to the USA. It is customary to tip between 10 and 15 percent on your restaurant bill. In most cases, a service charge is not included. In bars, $0.50-$1 per drink is acceptable. If you are having pizza delivered, tip the delivery person. Tip about $2 per bag to hotel porters and tip your taxi driver 10 percent. Hairdressers should also be tipped for good service.

Connectivity

Mobile Phones

Canada's mobile phone networks are compatible with networks in the USA, but different from most other networks around the world as it favors CDMA networks, rather than the GSM networks used in most of Europe, Asia and Africa. While this may be technologically convenient for visitors from the USA, there is still the matter of roaming fees, which can be expensive, even for US tourists. Some US service providers do offer special deals for calls from Canada, or the option to limit charges and usage to a pre-set daily rate. Only three Canadian service providers provide close to nationwide coverage. They are Rogers, Telus and Bell. Wind Mobile offers coverage mainly in the urban and semi-urban areas of Canada, but partners with other networks to make up the difference. Additionally, there are a number of regional services, such as Ice Wireless, which covers parts of Inuvik, Yukon and the Northwestern Territories, MTS Mobility in Manitoba, Sasktel Mobility in Saskatchewan, Vidéotron Mobile in Ottawa and Quebec and Eastlink on Canada's Atlantic seaboard.

Canada's mobile industry is geared mainly towards locals, with contracts being preferred over prepaid options and a Canadian credit card being mandatory for the activation of most mobile deals. However, the industry is slowly changing to meet the demands of tourists. Bell is Canada's oldest telephone company, but they have moved with the times. If your main priority is staying connected to the web, your best bet will be their data only sim card, available at about $9.95. You can top-up using a Bell recharge voucher. Rogers is the Canadian carrier that is most compatible with international networks. They offer free sims for the activation with a new phone purchase, but will charge $10 for a replacement sim if you have your own device. Once you have your sim card, you can choose from various usage plans starting at $30 or choose a pay-per-minute plan with minimum $10 top-ups and the option of data add-ons. Rogers is partnered with Fido and Chatr Mobile.

Dialing Code

The dialing code for Canada is +1, the same as the United States.

Emergency numbers

General Emergency: 911
MasterCard: 1 800 307 7309
Visa: 1 800 847 2911

General Information

Public Holidays

1 January: New Year's Day
March/April: Good Friday

1 July: Canada Day
First Monday in September: Labor Day
25 December: Christmas Day

Several public holidays are only observed in certain states. The official separation of Nunavut from the North-Western Territories is celebrated in Nunavut on the 9th of July. Quebec observes Easter Monday, National Patriot's Day (on the Monday preceding 25 May) and Jean Baptiste Day, also known as Quebec Day (24 June). Victoria Day falls on the Monday on or before 24 May and it is observed in all states except New Brunswick, Nova Scotia and Prince Edward Island. In the Northwest Territories, 21 June is a Provincial holiday celebrated as National Aboriginal Day. Discovery Day is celebrated in 3 states. In Newfoundland and Labrador, it falls on the Monday closest to 24 June and in Yukon, it is commemorated on the Monday nearest to 17 August. Thanksgiving is celebrated on the second Monday in October in most states, except for New Brunswick, Newfoundland, Nova Scotia and Prince Edward Island. Remembrance Day is observed in most states as a statutory holiday, with the exception of Manitoba, Nova Scotia, Ontario and Quebec. While special events like Mother's Day, Valentine's Day, Father's Day and Halloween are widely observed, they are not holidays. Although not a statutory holiday, Civic Day is observed on the first Monday of August in Alberta, British Columbia, New Brunswick, Nunavut, Ontario and Saskatchewan.

Time Zones

Canada is divided into six different time zones. Newfoundland Standard Time is used in the areas of Newfoundland and the south-eastern tip of Labrador. It can be calculated as Greenwich Mean Time/Co-ordinated Universal Time (GMT/UTC) -3 hours and 30 minutes in winter and -2 hours and 30 minutes in summer. Atlantic Standard Time is used in most of Labrador, New Brunswick, Nova Scotia, Prince Edward Island and Quebec. It is calculated as Greenwich Mean Time/Co-ordinated Universal Time (GMT/UTC) -4 hours in winter and -3 hours in summer. Eastern Standard Time (EST) applies in most of Nunavut, Ontario and Quebec and is calculated as Greenwich Mean Time/Co-ordinated Universal Time (GMT/UTC) -5 hours in winter and -4 hours in summer. Central Standard Time (CST) is observed in Manitoba, Saskatchewan and parts of Ontario and can be calculated as Greenwich Mean Time/Co-ordinated Universal Time (GMT/UTC) -6 hours in winter and -5 hours in summer. Mountain Standard Time (MST) is observed in Alberta, the Northwestern Territories, eastern communities in British Columbia, Lloydminster in Saskatchewan and Kugluktuk Cambridge Bay in Nunavut. It is calculated as Greenwich Mean Time/Co-ordinated Universal Time (GMT/UTC) -7 hours in winter. Pacific Standard Time (PST) applies in Yukon and most of British Columbia and can be calculated as Greenwich Mean Time/Co-ordinated Universal Time (GMT/UTC) -8 hours in winter and -7 hours in summer.

Daylight Savings Time

Clocks are set forward one hour at 01.00am on the last Sunday of March and set back one hour at 01.00am on the last Sunday of October for Daylight Savings Time. Most of the province of Saskatchewan (except Creighton and Denare Beach) does not observe Daylight Savings Time and neither do Pickle Lake, New Osnaburgh and Atikokan in Ontario, Quebec's North Shore, Southampton Island in Nunavut and Creston in British Columbia.

School Holidays

In Canada, the academic year runs from mid September to the latter part of June. There is a two week winter break in December and a two week spring break in March. In most provinces, the summer holidays begin on the last Saturday of June, although Quebec factors in the public holiday on 24 June. Schools begin again on the Tuesday after Labor Day.

Trading Hours

In Canada, trading hours are regulated at provincial level. In British Columbia, Alberta, and Saskatchewan, as well as Yukon, Northwestern Territories and Nunavut, there are no legislation prohibiting trade at any particular time, but trading hours will usually vary according to the area and the type of business. Common trading hours are from 10am to 6pm from Mondays to Saturdays, with shops also being open from noon to 5pm on Sundays. At larger city malls you can expect late trade on Thursdays, Fridays and Saturdays. In urban areas, there will usually be a pharmacy and convenience store trading 24 hours and some fast food outlets may also trade round the clock. Post Office hours may vary, according to the location of the outlet. In Quebec, shopping hours are set at 9.30am to 5.30pm from Mondays to Wednesdays, 9.30am to 9pm on Thursdays and Fridays, 9.30am to 5pm on Saturdays and 10am to 5pm on Sundays. In Nova Scotia, shops are closed on Remembrance Day, whereas in Manitoba, Quebec, Ontario, New Brunswick and Prince Edward Island, shops are closed on most major public holidays, including Remembrance Day. In those states, Sunday trading is also restricted.

Driving Policy

Canadians drive on the right side of the road. If you have a valid driver's license in your own country, you should be permitted to drive in Canada, but it may be advised that you apply for an International Driving Permit, which will include a translation of your licence in English and French. The minimum driving age is 16. To drive in Canada, car insurance is compulsory and you will be required to organize a policy that provides adequate cover for your age group and driving experience. If renting a car, check that car insurance is including in your rental agreement. All ten provinces in Canada have legislation restricting the use of mobile phones while driving and requires you to use a hands free kit. Speed limits are given in kilometers. In Canada, the speed limits are set at 110km per hour for multiple lane highways, 80km per hour for 2-lane highways, 60km per hour for urban and suburban roads, between 40 and 50km per hour for residential roads and 30km per hour for school zones.

Drinking Policy

In Canada, legislation regarding the sale and consumption of alcohol is set at the provincial level. In most provinces, the minimum drinking age is 19, with the exception of Alberta, Manitoba and Quebec, where you can legally drink from 18 years of age. An old law dating back to 1928 prohibits Canadians from transporting alcohol across provincial and national boundaries without permission from the provincial liquor control board. Do bear this in mind, if you are planning to travel through several provinces or territories with your own supply of beer or wine. It is against the law. Of the provinces, Quebec has the most relaxed liquor laws and allows alcohol sales from regular grocery stores.

Smoking Policy

Smoking legislation is determined at provincial level in Canada. All provinces adopted some form of restriction on smoking in public places and work spaces in the period between 2003 and 2008. In Nunavut, which has the highest percentage of smokers, it is illegal to smoke within 3 metres of a building's entrance. In Toronto, you may not smoke within 9 metres of a building's entrance. In Manitoba, Quebec, Saskatchewan, British Columbia, Nova Scotia, Ontario, New Brunswick, Newfoundland and Labrador, it is illegal to smoke in a vehicle if minors under the age of 16 are passengers. Alberta also restricts the type of outlets that are allowed to sell cigarettes.

Electricity

Electricity: 110 volts
Frequency: 60 Hz
Canada uses electricity sockets similar to those found in the USA, with two flat prongs or blades arranged parallel to each other. These are compatible with Type A and Type B plugs. You will also find that appliances from the UK or Europe which were designed to accommodate a higher voltage will not function as effectively in Canada. While a converter or transformer should be able to adjust the voltage, you may still experience some performance degradations with the type of devices that are sensitive to variations in frequency as the Canada uses 60 Hz, instead of the 50 Hz which is common in Europe and the UK.

Food & Drink

Breakfast in Canada can be a hearty mix of fried bacon, pork sausage, eggs, deep-fried potatoes, toast and pancakes, but continental twists such as French toast and pastries are equally popular, as is cereal. Lunch is generally a light meal such as sandwiches, salads or soup. Traditionally meat is central to the Canadian dinner. Canada also has its own range of tempting sweets and confectionaries. Maple syrup is a staple ingredient of various cookies and pastries. Canadian chocolate bars include the Coffee Crisp, made of coffee flavored wafers smothered in milk chocolate and the Nanaimo Bar, a British Columbian snack with with a rich buttery filling sandwiched between two slices of chocolate. The Beaver's Tail is a lump of deep-fried dough sprinkled with sugar and cinnamon. Poutine is a simple fast food that originated in Quebec and consists of French fries, smothered in cheese and gravy. Sometimes chicken, bacon, sausage, ground beef or other meat is added. Another French-Canadian favorite is Tourtière, or meat pies, usually made of beef, veal or pork. If you have trouble choosing between pizza and pasta, then the Pizza-ghetti is for you. It combines half a pizza with a helping of Spaghetti Bolognaise.

Canadian coffee culture embraces the simplicity of Tim Horton, the country's most popular chain of coffee and doughnut shops, but in recent years, tastes have grown somewhat more sophisticated and cosmopolitan. Bottled glacier water is available across Canada. Coke, Pepsi and Diet Coke are the best selling soft drinks, but for a taste of local flavor, try Jones Soda, which features a range of tastes including green apple, bubblegum, strawberry lime, crushed melon and even peanut butter and jelly. Some of their limited editions include pumpkin pie and poutine flavored soft drinks. Ginger ale is a Canadian invention and another Canadian favorite is clamato juice, a combination of clam chowder and tomato juice, which is combined with vodka to produce the Bloody Caesar, the country's signature cocktail.

Beer is Canada's favorite alcoholic beverage and Budweiser from across the border, its top selling brand. Canadian beer drinkers love to experiment, which accounts for the popularity of craft beers and also the introduction of ice beer amidst fierce rivalry by two of Canada's top beer brewers, Labatt and Molson. Both brands are based in the province of Quebec which has a lively beer brewing tradition and hosts two annual beer festivals, one in Quebec City and one in Montreal. Canadians also produce ice wine, a sweet dessert wine and rye whiskey, of which the award-winning Canadian Club and Crown Royal are its most representative brands.

Useful Websites

http://wikitravel.org/en/Canada
https://www.attractionscanada.com/
http://www.frontier-canada.co.uk/
http://www.canadianbucketlist.com/
http://transcanadahighway.com/
http://www.tour-guide-canada.com/

http://www.thecanadaguide.com/

Printed in Poland
by Amazon Fulfillment
Poland Sp. z o.o., Wrocław